T0198957

My Black History, My Character and Me

Dr. Angela Sims Stephens

Saddraid A. Hubbard, Illustrator

AuthorHouse™
1663 Liberty Drive
Bloomington, IN 47403
www.authorhouse.com
Phone: 1 (833) 262-8899

Because of the dynamic nature of the Internet, any web addresses or links contained in this book may have changed since publication and may no longer be valid. The views expressed in this work are solely those of the author and do not necessarily reflect the views of the publisher, and the publisher hereby disclaims any responsibility for them.

Any people depicted in stock imagery provided by Getty Images are models, and such images are being used for illustrative purposes only. Certain stock imagery © Getty Images.

This book is printed on acid-free paper.

ISBN: 978-1-4634-1754-3 (sc)

Print information available on the last page.

Published by AuthorHouse 07/23/2020

authorHOUSE®

This book is Dedicated to Kevin Jr.
With Love Mommy

AFRICA BORE PROSPEROUS KINGS AND QUEENS
WHERE BLACK MEN AND WOMEN WERE ESTEEMED WORTHY BEINGS

EUROPEANS CAME BY THE TWILIGHT OF NIGHT
AFRICANS THEN BECAME THEIR POSSESSION AND RIGHT

ONCE ON THE SALTY ATLANTIC OCEAN AND CARRIBEAN SEAS
MY GREAT GREAT GRANDPARENTS HAD SHACKLES AND NO KEYS

THEY CAME FROM THE MOTHERLAND BLACK RED AND GREEN
TO THE SHORES OF THE STATE VIRGINIA THE QUEEN

THESE AUNTS AND UNCLES WERE SLAVES FOR MANY MANY AND STILL
MANY YEARS
THEY WERE WHIPPED AND WORKED THROUGH BLOOD SWEAT AND TEARS

FREEDOM CAME THROUGH AMENDMENT THIRTEEN NOT FIRST PART
OF LAW
IT'S TAKING DECADES FOR THE ECHO TO REACH WITH THE OLIVE
BRANCH IN CLAW

CLASSIFIED THE COUNTRY WENT TO SEGREGATED SCHOOLS WITH
ONLY THE COLOR OF YOUR SKIN
THE WORLD OF THE SIXITIES WERE SEPARATED BY KINS

THE BRILLANT BLACKS EMERGED FROM TIME BACK IN THE DAY THEY STOOD TALL AND BOWED LOW AND DARED THOSE MADE FROM THE SAME CLAY

TODAY WE ARE SPECIAL THANKS TO THE ANCESTORS OF PAST
THEY MARCHED AND PREACH AND CALLED OUT FOR JUSTICE AT LAST

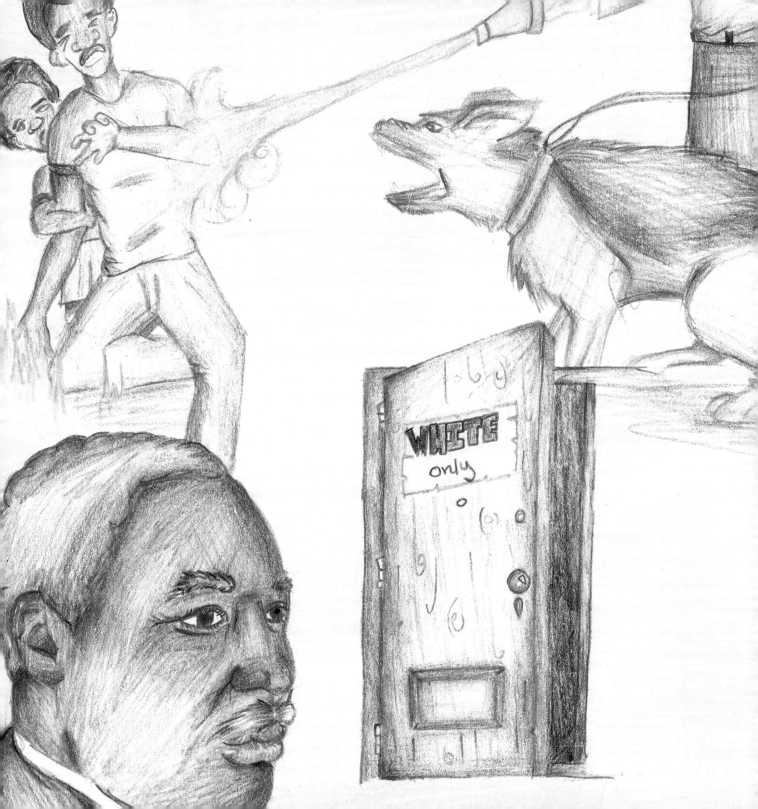

IN SCHOOL AND WITH FAMILY YOU SHOULD STUDY LISTEN AND LEARN
DO GOOD BY YOUR NEIGHBORS AND KNOWLEDGE YOU YEARN

FIGHTING AND BACKBITING BRUISE THE SKIN AND BREAK THE HEART
IT CAN LEAD YOU TO A DESTINY THAT IN LIFE IS NOT SMART

YOUR CHARACTER IS PART OF WHO YOU ARE AND REFLECT TO OTHERS
WONDERFUL COLORFUL CHARACTER IS A CELEBRATION OF LIFE'S
LOVERS

MOTHERS AND FATHERS OF HISTORY'S BREATH WHO LOVED BLED
SIGHED CRIED AND DIED
I SALUTE YOU I REMEMBER YOU IN CHARACTER I ABIDE

Printed in the United States
By Bookmasters